L'appel Du Vide

Regan Frioux

BookLeaf Publishing

India | USA | UK

Presentation by *BookLeaf Publishing*

Web: www.bookleafpub.com

E-mail: info@bookleafpub.com

ISBN: 9789358314496

First edition 2023

DEDICATION

To my mom, step-dad, and every single one of my friends. I love you.

ACKNOWLEDGEMENT

To my mom, thank you for forever being here and supporting me. When it felt as if others didn't support my outlandish choice of a career, you told me to jump. To my step-dad, really, thank you for stepping up. I know I always have a supporter in you guys, if nobody else.

To my best friend and soulmate, Anaia, thank you for giving me every single laugh I needed. Even from hundreds of miles away, you always have my back. (I miss you).

To Athena, thank you for giving in every single time I asked you to look over these poems. Not even just these, but every essay or story that I sent you, I am so thankful that you were there to fix my mess.

To my friends in College (there's too many to list here), thank you all for being the best friends ever. We are all drowning in assignments, always, but you never fail to step away from yourselves to make sure that I am doing okay.

Chorophobia

I'm scared of the stars and how they shine too
bright
I'm scared of the sun rising in the night
I'm scared of the constant beeping of a heart
And I'm scared that it'll stop and I'll just fall
apart

I'm afraid of losing those who I love
So in my thoughts I hold their hands
And put a staple through the palms

I'm spun around by madness
It twirls me around and kicks me down
A swirling, devouring blackness

An irreplaceable love
Brought forth by chance
Voice forbidden
Thoughts forced hidden
You just told me to dance

Head held high
Leaping and twirling
A structure of perfect poise I string
Symphonies of broken laws

"All I do is try."

Waiting in the wings
Crowds cheer on
Beating their feet
Waiting for the curtain's call

But where are you
Lights blind my eyes
Where are you?
What is a dancer to get paid with lies?

I am cloaked in darkness
And shoved into a box
With crystal clear walls
And a keyless lock

But then there is you
You plucked stars from the sky
I watch them explode in your palm
The one attached to mine

But then there is you
Won't you help to set me free
I face your back
Your feet pound on
I watch until you're all but gone.

I'm scared of the sharp edges of a smile

I'm scared of the sudden pierce of bile
I'm scared of the shadows of empty rooms
And I'm scared of the death of love forced into a
tomb

Red Rosary

Candles burn out
They drip and melt until nothing is left
of reality, Blurred by red wine
spilt across new and old and blue

Wax smeared on cold skin
Down the dip of a concave cheek
Softened by guilt, are the lines on my face
Is the gray of your eyes

"Take them out"- as if they are pearls
To be collected
As if they might look pretty strung around my
neck
Around my fist, clenched in prayer
A cross dangling just above failed epiphanies

"Take them out."
But oh, what a pretty price they would catch
If I were to sell them

Lost in a forest of vines and moss
Tangling me into a hug,
Green water kissing at my feet
Is what I used to see

But, oh, they are different now
Grey and sunken
Not nearly as valuable

God watches me mourn
He watches my hands string along lace curtains
Watches as my eyes, still valuable, search for
your soul
Willing to find it alive, vowing to have and to
hold

God watched when you dropped to your knees
in prayer
Hands grasping for repent
Rose petals pouring out of your throat
That sings out his name

Whispers imitate you
"Take them from me"
 But God watches me too closely
Too far within me
To know what I have already stolen

Dear, I cannot take any more from you
No matter how much you will me to

Overconciousness

The day we open our eyes
We are everything and nothing at once.
Sobbing lumps of clay to be shaped and carved
Into something worthwhile.
Briefly, we are all things we can be
Briefly, we are marvelous
How can we truly come to terms
With the meaning of life larger than reality
What is destiny? If not the reality of change
A metamorphosis of the soul- what it itself
decides is marvelous
Forget yourself, rediscover it. Discover
What your soul wants you to find.
Find what is meant to be unearthed.
An X carved into your sternum.
This, a part of life not fated.
Instead, this is aimless.
Shooting stars.
Guided by gravity.
Stars embroider the sky,
Bound to explode billions of years later.
A thousand shining stitches,
The hands of fate, pricked by too many needles.
Black holes, untouchable, until one day they
aren't.

The gods above, slotting pieces into place.
"Check", life stutters for just a moment.
"Checkmate", a planet dies.
Briefly, we are marvelous.
Until a god tries to catch a human soul.
A child grasps at fireflies,
Crushing light between his clumsy fingers.
Crushing a human soul that changes not with the
phases of the moon
Or conjointly with the tides of the sea.
But rapidly it gathers pieces of
An unknown puzzle.

Ever consuming tempts

He is unknown, the night,
A killer among shadows.
Bleeds from his eyes, his cloak, his estate
The dusk of days overshadowed by the moon.

He is a mirror, two sided
Of melted silver that weeps down
Intricately carved, hardened edges
One he cannot touch
And one he does not reflect within

He stood at the forefront of my being
Unmoving, uninvited
Whisked away by the flare of morning
Always to return the very next night

He stood there awaiting
A flash in my eyes
Invitation to cross the line between
Life and death

When I awake the next morning
A burning sensation runs down into the pit of
my lungs
It spits up its venom into my throat

And scratches out my tonsils

He is inside,
Sitting next to me
An apple in his palm
With a bite carved out

He is the red that flows through me
Drips from my neck
Into a pool consuming—
Eating away at my feet

I write to you, hear my plea
Beware of the night and the songs he sings
His shadows spread, eating away
And leaving a crimson trail in his wake

He is unseen, the night
A killer among the shadows
He slithers amidst the lack of light
His whispers are quiet
But they demand of your life

As I sit, withering in a foreign land
The one eclipsed with forever night
I think of you, the life you hold
Of brilliant ideas and smiles
Shooting rays of sun into the darkest parts of me

I write to you, as shadows threaten
To engulf my very being
I write to you, in solemn prayer,
That he will avoid your sunlit life

He is gone, from me
And onto the next.
Beware his tricks, his tempts
Of the tales he strings
But remember my name
As I fall to the depths.

Flying upside down

The sun melts onto my nose bridge
Sticking baby hairs to my neck
The wind is cool, at least
With it, it brings the scent of the sea
Feet tumble on gravel roads
Racing to the cliffs before the sun leaves its peak

I am the swan
Diving from rocky edges
Soaring through the air
Wind slicing through me
Ripping euphoric cries
From my vocal chords
Tearing at my strings, unraveling

A freefall dance
Gravity's grip, released
Hands uselessly reaching out
Grabbing at the remains of summer
Before the seasons shift to fall

And when I fall apart
Hitting the water
Spreading across the surface like scattered petals
Submerging into a void

Echoed laughter from above
The tides grab onto my threads
Dragging me downwards

Trembling figures above stare down
Remembering back, just minutes before
Their hands pushing, shoving
Pressing heavy fingers into malleable skin
Tossing me over the edge
Assuming that I will float
Hoping I will sink

Looking upwards
The water ripples across
My sinking form
Blurring my existence
Until I rest at the very bottom
A still image, a statue of history

We killed the sun

When the sea misses the moon, she looks
upwards
Reaching out in tenacious waves
Towards the sky, stained black ink
And there she will find, the moon drawing
her in

Thunder across the expanse of nothing
That nothing has ever became yet
Density released into millions of atoms
Destiny to become the expanse of
everything

Before her, or before the actuality of her
There were her parents
Stuffing wads of money into shredded envelopes
Dropping bags into rivers, sinking like silver
Before him, or before
the actuality of him
There were his parents
Scrambling for loose
change

                         Picking bags of wealth
from rivers
Whisked away, a tornado of fear, into an
unknown land
Strangers speak syllables unknown to her
Padding along the splintered wood of a deck
So hungry, longing, the sea bites at the gunwale
Loving splashes bash away her little legs
Sea glass eroded away by the waves
Until her body, every atom, gives way to gravity
                         Someone has fallen, he
hears the crowd screeching
                         prayers
                         Melodic bird calls,
overlapping and battling
                         He grips his mother's
hand,
                         His tiny fingers soon
crushed her grip
                         She whisks him away, a
tornado of fear, that he will slip
                         too
Her schoolbooks, erupting from her bag
Earth trembles beneath her
Buildings crack, tumbling to the floor
Her books, stranded beneath rubble and ash
As her legs dart away, a deer from prey
                         Exploring the rubble of
last night's attack

                    His arms scrape along
jagged edges
                    Rocks form mountains
around abandoned storefronts
                    A breeze brushes the
knots from his hair
                    Sweeping dust across
his face
                    And a piece of paper
into his hand
                    A picture of a hoofed
creature, eyes wide, deep
She skips over to the abandoned storefront
Glass clouded by judgements
Clouded by breath, peaking through
Attention stumped by a smudge to her right
                    His fingertips drag
along walls
                    Eyes glued to the
crumbled floor
                    Waiting for a crack to
open and eat him whole
                    His fingertips stop upon
a window
                    Dust puddles around his
fingers,
                    Pushing it around like
the tide
                    He draws a picture

To her right is a smudge, sloppy swipes
Stamped with fingerprints
The image of a fish
Surrounded by a sea of absolutely nothing
Nowhere to settle down, nowhere to call home
                      The sky claps,
deafening applause
                      Fire rains down directly
after
                      To his left there is a
screech
                      Around a corner, there
is a girl
Rumbling ground,
Falling walls
Her legs push her, past the lonely fish
Into the obscurity of an alley
Into the warmth of a boy

    The heavens screech
    Above them
    Huddled against the other
    As rocks pelt against his cheeks
    Cratering his face
    His arms, bruised, shielding her

    Walking along the rubble
    Tumbling over rocky shorelines
    Feet sticking to carved boulders

She tumbles and he guides her along
Walking together, back to wherever home
might be

Bombs drop again and again
Shattering homes and lives
He wades to her, amidst it all

As she finishes her studies
As he swipes from pockets
Enough coins to scavenge
Bolts and metal
An energy source powerful enough to kill
the sun

For if the sun is gone, so is everyone else
So is the war and the place with no place to
go
The big expanse of water
That they plod through, looking for a home

Lights flicker on
Glaring bright, like the bride on her
wedding day
A star could not stand to be outstaged
Lights flicker off
As the beam stretches out
Breaking through the atmosphere
Cracking through a glass bubble

Lights flicker out,
The sun breathing its last breath, fizzling to
nothing
Her hand in his
Crushing bone, clinging on

The anger of the sun, raging over the
surface of the earth
Stampeding, trampling over life
The only known source of it
So angry, the sun
Its rage consuming the love of the two
Forcing them apart
That she became the sea, and he became the
moon

Memor(ial)ized

Every night I wander these halls. I could map them out
in my sleep. I know where the carpet crinkles up
between uneven
floorboards. I know where my favorite books sit
on their shelves.
I know there is a chair in the corner to my right,
overused,
leather peeling off, littered into the cracks of
creaking wood.

 Yesterday, there was someone new sitting in
that chair. He spoke
to me about my favorite books, like he already
knew. He must have
already known. His neck arched down,
forcefully, uncomfortably–
eyes scanning over faded words.

Today, when I wander, I go tumbling to the
floor. The carpet
is snarled up, catching my foot unknowing. My
brain reels,
a sense of familiarity in this sequence. This
carpet, however,

has never looked so different. The man sitting in
the chair today,
looking at me with worry in his sagging eyes, I
have never seen
before.

Today, when I wander, the shelves are all out of
place. A maze,
A librarian's labyrinth, locking me into endless
circles of disarray. Somebody
has moved my sacred place around to mess with
me,
I'm sure of it. I'm sure that my favorite novel sat
on the shelf
just before me, but now it is nowhere to be
found.

The cover brown, or maybe it was blue, and the
title– well, that's
not too important. But, surely, it was right here.
And surely, that chair in
the corner has never been there before. And
surely, the man sitting in it is a stranger to me.
Why is his smile so warm, so welcoming?

The arms of war, hold me so dear

Love is a war, a conflict of time
Metal shards slice through cold air,
reminiscent of the morning before life.
This is the day after death.

You are sprawled, feet kicking morning rays away
Arms wrapped around me tightly
Droplets of dust sprinkle across fresh air
Floating around still figures
Of you and I, together, within a sea of warmth

Flares of rockets, erupting into fiery prisms
Bursts echo off of the clouds
Cheers of nationality
Triumph over bloodshed

You are sprawled, buried beneath the dirt
Arms mere scraps of bone
Droplets of dust sprinkle across stale air
Floating around still figures
Of you beneath a sea of cold

Furies of fire illuminating the horizon

Outrunning the sun
Triumphing over life
Hitting the ground with fervor

Metal shards slice through cold air,
Floating over violent peace.
Memories lost to the barrel of a gun
A soul clouded by gunpowder.

There was a day, lit by the deep hour of
June
When nothing was right, between you and I
There was a day that you held me in your
arms
This day that the sun screamed at us-
"It burns, it burns"
Screaming through the air is the missile that
tore you from your huddle
Into the air, burning through the atmosphere
Burning through the wings on your back
Until you hit the ground, falling through, six
feet

Variations of time

A breath breaks free from cracked lips,
slowly, for the first time.
Hands creep up, wrapping
around my throat. Threaten
the breath back in. Shoving it down,
until it expands in my lungs. They pop,
like balloons.
                        Scratching at my throat,
fingernails
                        carving deep lines, veins. A
breath caught
                        at the back of my throat,
deep and heavy.
                        It threatens to slice me open,
                        disintegrate my lungs-
                        Burning a hole from the
inside out.
Pounding at the walls of an hourglass.
The grains stick to my skin, drying me out.
What was a drizzle becomes a downpour,
time running out, days becoming hours.
                        It's up to my jaw now, a
threat of streaming
                        into my mouth, stuffing my
organs full like taxidermy.

But the glass cracks on its
own

Sand pouring out,
unearthing me.

Motherly arms, hold me to
the light.

Reborn again.
A bird flies overhead. I am reaching
out my hand. Except that, it can fly and
I cannot. Bound to the ground– glass walls,
a room surrounded in two way mirrors. Watched
like a hawk, my every move.

A key, pressed into my
palm. Warm hands

stretching over mine. The
same palms that

bloom open, extending
towards an exit.

A staircase, down the
brainstem, out of delusion.

Without an encore

I close my eyes, and the moon falls from the sky.
Symphonic melodies of your whispers in my ear.
Soft, decrescendo, a timbre singing pretty
promises.
Where is the cut off, why does this keep
repeating?
You are the maestro, pulling me every which
way—
Your arms fly up: grasping at my face, ripping
out my hair,
digging out my teeth. The reeds weep high
strung chords
in the front row. A personal audience, they
watch on, intently,
as your hands flick upwards in a downbeat— my
beating heart,
accelerando. You fall into time with me, our
breaths,
our lips. You are the bass that speeds up, and I
must follow you.
Except I can't, because my eyes are closed. I
can't see
your hands, frantically grasping at the moon.
Flying

this way and that, instructing the highs and lows to merge
once more. But they just won't. A cacophony of deafening notes, too sharp. They howl without a will to follow.
I can taste the blood on your lip– where is the reprise?
I can feel your lungs skip over breaths, hands falling
from the sky, scattering music around us.
When I open my eyes, there you are, all laid out before me.
A band without a beat, an orchestra without its maestro.

Taking up space

Squeeze me tight,
'Til I explode
These chains of silk
Gently sewn

Into the bodice
Of my dress
Create the curve
That you'll caress

Taut strings tug
Ensnare my wrists
Every which way I
Turn and twist

It stings- just a bit
A needle in your grasp
A pearl of blood
You Swallow my gasp
Push my chin back
Straighten my spine
Wrap another silk
Around me like a vine

Until it overgrows

Across my porcelain face
Mold me in a way
To decorate your space

Please call if you have any information

Into the forest the small dog wanders.
Invited by the howling wind.
It is snowing and she curls up under a bush.
Thin branches helpless against the wind.
Blanketed in that bitter cold, the dog falls asleep.

(Have you seen her?)

The next morning, snow has piled inches high.
If the dog were still alive, she would curl her
small body tighter.
Or she might get up and run away to find some
warmth.
As things go, however, the snow continues to
pile up.

Autopsy

Rain drops brush through his hair
Sticking to his eyelashes
Wetting his lips
His chest expands and collapses,
His cheeks are red, warm
He is alive
But doesn't he look peaceful?
If he woke up,
Eyes flickering wide,
Then squinting, blocking the rain.
Rain over his warm skin,
A gloss. A topcoat over
The last layer of paint.
Isn't it just beautiful?
His chest expands and collapses
Heart clawing against iron bars
He is alive, awake, viable.
Instead, his eyes are shut.
His face is still.
I wonder, examining him
With a doctors scope,
Is this what he looks like in death?
Could I take a blade,
Carve out each organ,
And keep them in my fridge?

The clouds pass,
The rain stops,
His eyes open,
I put the knife back into my pocket.

Uncherished

To be alone is to be a bird with clipped wings.
A bird, locked away in a cage.
Bars of metal, branching up.
Singing its summer song-
Mechanical, rehearsed.
Crescendo of the abandoned.
Around him is paradise,
An expanse of white space.
Alone in time, in light, in existence.
Look again, two birds in the cage.
Around them is a cosmos so dense–
So unwound–
That nobody can see through.
To be forgotten is to blend into the foliage.
Sometimes people pass by
Tuning out their yearning song.
Two birds, overlooked.
All too focused on unfinished art, unsolved
equations.
To be together is two birds with clipped wings.
Celestial sky surrounds them,
alone, together.

Terrified

There is a kissing bug on my wall,
Large, oval shaped–
Slowly stalking,
Towards nowhere in particular.
I watch it slowly, steadily,
Each creep and crawl.
It waits until the night,
Until my eyes grow too weak,
Fluorescents too bright,
To focus on him.
He flutters of the wall,
And tucks me into bed.
Kiss me, gently, to sleep.
Curse me, with a bite.

There is a ladybug on my wall,
They say,
Ladybugs bring good luck.
But ladybugs also bring
Other ladybugs.
When I squash one
Beneath my shoe
(screaming, probably),
They ooze out a yellowish blood,
(spewing, I'd imagine).

The other ladybugs tell me,
This blood smells divine.
For now there are 3 ladybugs on my wall.

There is a bee on my wall.
Resting her roundish body.
After a long day-
Cleaning, cooking, watching the kids.
Thank goodness she kicked him out.
Or killed him, rather.
Nevertheless,
Better by herself,
Floating amidst a field of
Flowers.
Make some honey for me,
Perhaps we could catch flies.
More bugs for my wall.

Kingdom

Beth liked to play in the sand, in the fall, when
the wind kicked up a bit.
Not on a beach, but confined to a sandbox.
Shoving tiny hands up to her wrists in piles of
sand,
Molding a castle with a mote. Fingerprints
indent
Where the windows would be– the door.

Beth was my friend, always waiting for me in
the sandbox.
Like she never left, she was always there,
waiting.
Quietly– she never spoke– she played with her
sand
And listened to my stories.

I remember, last week
I brought Beth a can of soda.
Begged Mom to buy me an extra. Mom looked
at me funny.
Questioning eyes– I never drink more than one
can.
Beth never touched that soda, didn't even look at
it.

It sat there, fizzling out, until the sun went down and Mom
Dragged me home. And Beth stayed there.

I don't think Mom likes Beth very much.
I bring her up sometimes, I tell Mom about the
Castles we constructed. Mom makes this weird face
When I do. Nose scrunching, eyes avoiding me.
Now that I think of it, Mom always overlooks Beth.
She never says hi, steps on Beth's hand when it lays in the sand.
Almost as if she doesn't exist.

Everything is burning

Get down from there!
I can see the smoke,
Rising from your skin–
Pale as the moon–
Like a torch.
You sway,
Basking in the sun
On a cliff's edge.

Come back to me!
It's like your ears perk
At my voice. A dog
Hearing her name being called.
Bounding over to me,
Following a trail of candy
I left on the ground
Like a little kid, starved,
Away from the fire.

Step into me!
I leave the blinds closed,
During the day.
I live in darkness for you.
My eyes adjust to see your

Floating figure in the halls
At late hours, peeking through
Blackout curtains, for a
sweet taste of the moon.

Breathe me in!
I lie for you,
When gory bodies
Litter our floor.
When I have to mop up,
Pools of blood,
And save it for you
To drink later.

Spit me out!
I starve for you.
For a nourished body
Is far too alluring.
Far too tempting.
As much as I would enjoy
My neck within your jaws,
Unhinged like a lion.

Spit me out!
Above us is a parasol
Red, you chose it.
Rays of the sun spill down
Around us.

The burns on your skin
Begin to welt, raising up,
Pleading for attention.
But now you are safe.

Shadows bleed too

You could not have known the way I loved him.
As if the sun was suffocating, stealing air away
from the sky,
Pulsating, burning, picking away at my eyes
With a dull knife–utterly inefficient.
So what, if I cannot love him?
If the sun is to collapse in seven billion years
Efficiently shattering the earth into pieces no
larger than dust,
Then time is limited anyhow.
But we still lean on her for light, do we not?
In this case, I am the earth, in a constant
Whirling orbit around him.
Whereas he attracts more than just the earth,
He has the capacity for much more than just me.
For Venus and Jupiter and Pluto as well.
The lives of others crushed between his fingers,
a mere speck
Against a large orb of fire.
So be it, take him away, and let me return to the
moon's face.

Tea party

I've fallen down deep within
A place that rips my paper skin
Ashy rain and a spider lace
I'm stuck within the mad place.

Yowling echoes off the peaks
Of big large roundish, rosy cheeks
Face that paints a striking guise
Illuminate a pair of eyes.

Blinking up, big greed globes
Crawling foliage, arachnophobes
Bubbling, itching, beneath my skin
He disappears leaving just a grin.

Mix the pot of inky red
Watch out for the flying head
Bleeding on to holy roses
Wait until the mistress dozes.

As if my freckles grow into seeds
Birds pick them off like little beads
For a necklace to offer up
Place it into the Mad Queen's cup.

A plea to sing a lullaby
To my racing heart, sing a lie
Grab my lungs by their scruff
Til they go limp with one last puff.

Fossils

43

Arched necks, painful.
Unknown species gaping up at
A star much larger than the rest,
Quaking against a shadowy canvas.
It's hot, much hotter than usual.
But the stars have always been
Pretty.
Let's look at it for longer,
Even as the fire overtakes us.

Just wait until the end, mom.

When I was nine years old, my mother
sat me down and effectively ruined
my life. My hands in hers-- the last time
I felt her wedding ring digging into me- and she
told me about separation. Real separation.
The kind that ruptures a bond between two
people
so vast that no bridge could ever cross it.

But my father was there too, where is the blame
for him?
I can't remember his face, but I know he didn't
cry.
He held me later– when I was crying– and then
disappeared for weeks. He returned, and we
returned
(not to any sort of normalcy), but just to life.

My father had a special skill: sculpting.
(he never had time for much else,
being in the military). He knew how to forge
smiles out of my face, molding me like clay,
made sure that nobody else would know.

And then I was fourteen, a game of hide and
seek.
A threat bigger than I had ever known- hiding
into
the embrace of my mother. A place he would
never
check. She fixed me up– remolded me.

And then I was eighteen– moving away for
college,
for a job, for a life, for a wedding ring. Packing
clothes I would probably never wear into big
blue bags.
Leaving childhood, my mother. Separation. I
remember when she sat
me down, each and every time, and effectively
saved my life.
Tall figure, overshadowing me, protecting.

This separation, I could cross.